TRAGEDY AT SEA

TRAGEDY
AT SEA

THE SINKING OF
THE TITANIC

DAVID LONG

ILLUSTRATED BY
STEFANO TAMBELLINI

union
square
kids

NEW YORK

In memory of Captain Jack Irwin
of the Duke of Lancaster

union square kids

NEW YORK

UNION SQUARE KIDS and the distinctive Union Square Kids logo
are trademarks of Union Square & Co., LLC.

Union Square & Co., LLC, is a subsidiary of Sterling Publishing Co., Inc.

Text © 2021 David Long
Cover and interior illustrations © 2021 Stefano Tambellini

First published in Great Britain in 2021 by Barrington Stoke Ltd. First
published in the United States and Canada in 2024 by Union Square Kids.

ISBN 978-1-4549-5486-6

Library of Congress Control Number: 2023942899

For information about custom editions, special sales, and premium
purchases, please contact specialsales@unionsquareandco.com.

Printed in China

Lot #:
2 4 6 8 10 9 7 5 3 1

12/23

unionsquareandco.com

Cover design by Melissa Farris

Union Square & Co.'s EVERYONE CAN BE A READER books are expertly written,
thoughtfully designed with dyslexia-friendly fonts and paper tones, and carefully
formatted to meet readers where they are with engaging stories that encourage
reading success across a wide range of age and interest levels.

CONTENTS

TITANIC

LIFEBOATS & DAVITS: there was room for 64 lifeboats on the *Titanic* but only 20 were fitted; davits are a type of crane used to lower the lifeboats

STERN: back of the ship

RUDDER: a large blade that moved from side to side to steer the ship

PROPELLERS: the *Titanic* had three large propellers that pushed the ship through the water

FUNNELS: three of the funnels were the ship's chimneys, which allowed steam and smoke to escape from the engines; the fourth funnel was said to be for ventilation

CROW'S NEST: a small platform high up on the ship where the lookouts were stationed

BRIDGE: the control room of the ship

HULL: the main body of the ship

ANCHOR: a huge, heavy metal hook that could be lowered to the seabed to stop the ship from moving

BOW: front of the ship

1

THE RACE ACROSS THE OCEAN

Just over a hundred years ago, the only way to travel from Europe to America was by sea. There were no airplanes that could fly such a long way without landing to refuel.

But although you couldn't fly between Europe and the United States, transatlantic travel was already big business. Shipowners made enormous profits carrying rich people between the two continents. As well as very rich people, poor migrants wanted to start new lives on the other side of the ocean in America, so there was a lot of travel to and fro.

Two of the biggest shipping companies were the White Star Line and Cunard. These were both based in Liverpool in the north of England and competed with each other to attract passengers to the fastest, most lavish oceangoing liners that the world had ever seen.

Transatlantic ships had to be luxurious because the richest travelers expected the very best. Wealthy passengers would pay much more to travel in a ship that offered the space and comforts they enjoyed at home than in one that didn't.

The best liners had comfortable cabins as well as large saloons or lounges. Their elegant restaurants served fine food and wine, and some of the ships even had swimming pools and libraries where passengers could relax during the long voyage.

Speed was also important. Crossing the Atlantic by ship could take a week or more. Passengers on even the most luxurious liners wanted to get there quickly, especially if they were traveling on urgent or important business.

The ship that made the fastest crossing could win a prize called the Blue Riband. White Star and Cunard were both determined to win. Both companies knew they could charge even more for their most expensive cabins if they could prove that one of their vessels could reach America in less time than it took their rivals.

For many years the record for the fastest speed passed between different shipping companies. A total of 25 British ocean liners won the Blue Riband; a few of them won more than once. Five German ships were also successful, as were three American ones. Italy and France won it only once each.

The competition between the companies was extremely fierce as first one captain and then another raced to break the record. Cunard looked like it was about to move into first place in 1906 when it launched two huge new ships called the *Lusitania* and the *Mauretania*.

The company said that these two ships were faster and more luxurious than any of the ones operated by the White Star Line. They were right—both ships went on to win the Blue Riband. The *Lusitania* managed to break the record an impressive four times, and the *Mauretania* would go on to hold on to it for nearly 20 years. The *Mauretania* was also the biggest ship ever built anywhere in the world.

The White Star Line was desperate not to be left behind. They had already won several Blue Ribands, and Joseph Bruce Ismay, the head of the company, decided that he didn't need another one. Now he didn't want to make his ships faster—he wanted to do something different.

Ismay was sure that the best way to compete with the giant "Cunarders" was to build three new ships that were bigger than even the *Lusitania* or the *Mauretania*. Ismay wanted to offer his passengers more space, more comfort, and even more luxury than they would find on any of Cunard's ships.

In 1907 Ismay had a meeting with Lord Pirrie, the boss of an important shipyard in the north of Ireland called Harland and Wolff. For nearly 40 years, most White Star Line vessels had been built at Harland and Wolff's shipyard in Belfast, and over dinner one evening Ismay told Pirrie he was thinking of ordering three gigantic new ones. He wanted to call them the *Olympic*, the *Britannic*, and the *Titanic*. No one knew it yet, but one of them would go on to become the most famous ship of all time.

2

BUILDING THE GIANTS

The person who was going to design the new ships at Harland and Wolff was Thomas Andrews. He and his team drew up highly detailed plans for three magnificent-looking vessels. They had ten decks, and four funnels that were taller than a six-story block of apartments.

The new ships were about one and a half times bigger than the *Mauretania*. Each ship would be as long as three soccer fields (nearly 886 feet) and weigh more than 51,000 tons.

Ismay was excited by the huge size of the new vessels and told Lord Pirrie how impressed he was by the designs. He agreed to pay Harland and Wolff a total of about $3.8 million dollars to build the first two ships. This was an enormous sum of money in 1907—about the same as $440 million dollars today.

Harland and Wolff was one of the largest shipyards in Europe. More than 10,000 people worked in its Belfast yard while Lord Pirrie was in charge. The company had already built an astonishing 399 oceangoing vessels, but this new project was its greatest challenge so far.

The new White Star Line ships were so much larger than anything else they had built that the company had to change the layout of the entire yard to make room for the first two liners. Work on the third, the *Britannic*, had to wait. First, Harland and Wolff had to finish work on the *Olympic* and the *Titanic* and launch both ships out to sea.

The shipyard converted three large slipways into two even larger ones. Slipways are wide ramps that run down to the water, and they are mostly made of concrete. New ships are built on dry land and then "slipped" down the ramp and into the water when the main body or hull is watertight.

Harland and Wolff's slipways were already some of the biggest in the world, but the two new ones had to be really strong to take the weight of the *Olympic* and the *Titanic*. So before any of the work could begin, the ramps were covered with a solid layer of specially reinforced concrete nearly five feet thick.

Another important task was to build an immense gantry over the two slipways. This was a network of steel girders like a giant climbing frame. It was needed to support the cranes that had to lift heavy components and move them into position. Like almost everything else to do with the *Titanic*, the gantry at Harland and Wolff was the biggest anyone had ever seen.

The new gantry was more than 820 feet long and 229 feet high and weighed approximately 6,600 tons. (Most family cars are only about 2,200 pounds.) It was wide enough for both ships to fit beneath it, and it used a system of mechanical cranes and four large, electrically powered lifts for moving men and machinery.

Amazingly, this same gantry was still in use more than 50 years later. It towered over the city of Belfast until the 1960s and could be seen from many miles away.

A big ship's hull (its body) is usually made by attaching thick steel plates to a steel frame that looks a bit like the ribs of a skeleton. The work is slow and very dangerous because almost every component is large and immensely heavy.

The *Titanic*'s anchor was so heavy it needed 20 horses just to move it. The steel plates were so thick (nearly an inch in parts) that a single one could weigh several tons. Each one had to be put into precisely the right position before highly skilled workers could attach it to the frame using iron and steel rivets.

Rivets look a bit like short, thick nails and more than 6 million of them were used to build the first two ships. Every single rivet had to

be hammered into place to fix the plates to the steel frames safely. This is hard, skilled work, and it has been estimated that if one person had had to do the job on their own it would have taken them more than 300 years to hammer in all the rivets!

Harland and Wolff weren't trying to build the world's fastest ocean liners; the head of the White Star Line had decided these ships would be the biggest and most luxurious but not the fastest. Even so, the engines for the *Olympic* and the *Titanic* still had to be extremely powerful. At the time, these ships were the largest moving objects ever built, and three massive propellers were needed to get each of them moving.

Each vessel was fitted with a pair of huge steam engines to drive two of its three propellers. These main engines were as large as a three-story house and produced a total of 30,000 horsepower between them.

(A modern Formula One car produces less than 1,000 horsepower.) A slightly smaller engine called a steam turbine was used to turn the third propeller, and two others moved the 99-ton rudder from side to side to steer the ship.

The propellers, also known as "screws," were impressive. The left and right ones were nearly 23 feet wide and weighed 38 tons each. That's about the same weight as six adult

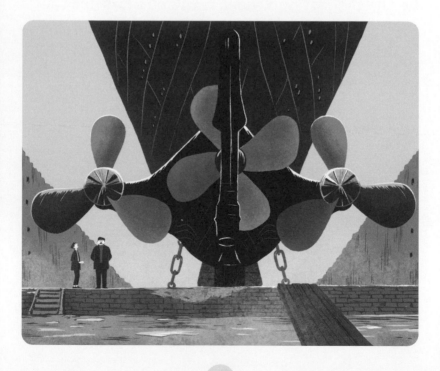

elephants (or seventy polar bears!). The middle
screw was very slightly smaller, and all three
were made of the same strong metal, an alloy
or mixture called manganese bronze.

Steam for the engines came from a
series of huge boilers that were heated up by
burning ordinary coal. The *Titanic* had around
160 furnaces and burned so much coal every
day (more than 880 tons) that 6,600 tons of it
had to be loaded onto the ship before a voyage
could begin. If you had to deliver that much
coal to a ship today, you'd need about 200 of
the largest trucks allowed on Britain's roads.
But when the *Titanic* was getting ready for its
launch, more than a hundred years ago, trucks
were much, much smaller.

3

"THE QUEEN OF THE SEAS"

The two enormous ships took several years to build and the *Olympic* was the first to set sail. It began its first voyage in June 1911 from southern England to New York City.

A few weeks before this, more than 100,000 people had turned out to see the *Titanic* slide down the giant slipway in Belfast and into the water for the first time.

Nearly 22 tons of slimy soap and animal fat had been slapped over the slipway to help the heavy ship slide down into the water more easily. Even so, it still took 62 seconds for *Titanic* to reach the water.

Almost immediately, the new ship was nicknamed "the Queen of the Seas" because

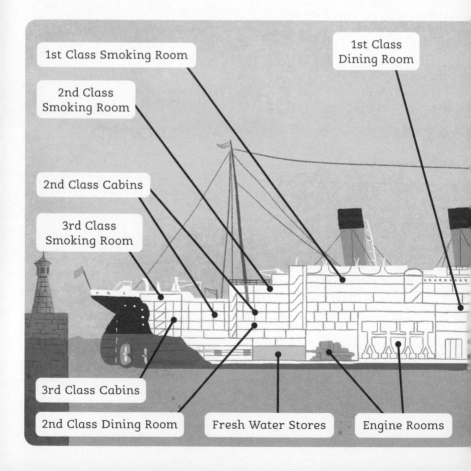

1st Class Smoking Room

1st Class Dining Room

2nd Class Smoking Room

2nd Class Cabins

3rd Class Smoking Room

3rd Class Cabins

2nd Class Dining Room

Fresh Water Stores

Engine Rooms

of its size and incredibly high levels of luxury. Work on the *Titanic* would now continue until its maiden voyage the following year.

The *Titanic* could hold more than 2,400 passengers, and they were divided into three different sections, depending on how much they had paid for their tickets.

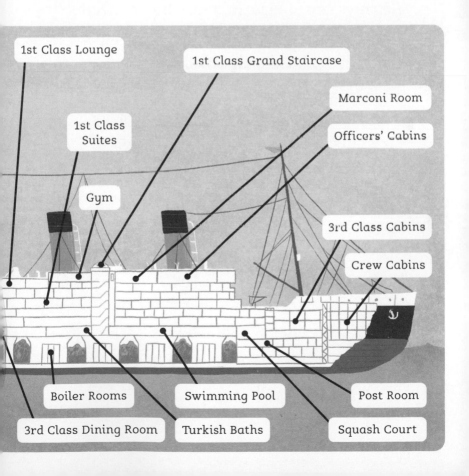

1st Class Lounge

1st Class Grand Staircase

Marconi Room

1st Class Suites

Officers' Cabins

Gym

3rd Class Cabins

Crew Cabins

Boiler Rooms

Swimming Pool

Post Room

3rd Class Dining Room

Turkish Baths

Squash Court

The most luxurious first-class suites cost up to $1,100 per person for the journey from Britain to America. This was more than fifteen years' salary for many ordinary people, and in 1912 it was possible to buy a new house for less than $250. Second-class tickets were a lot cheaper at $15, while third-class tickets cost only $10.

As the *Titanic* was so much bigger than any other ship, the White Star Line was able to equip it with many things to do on all of its ten decks. The best were reserved for people traveling in first or second class, but those in third class had their own relaxation area with a piano where they could enjoy musical evenings and sing-alongs.

While other shipowners expected these poorest passengers to bring their own food on board, on the *Titanic* they had their own dining room. This served cooked breakfasts and, at other times, large portions of soup, roast beef, fresh fruit, cheese, and pickles. Bread was freshly baked every day, and there was even a separate comfortable room for anyone in third class who wanted to smoke.

Meals in the dining room were free (and much better quality than the food many passengers could afford to eat at home), but third-class cabins were very basic, as well as noisy and cramped.

These cabins were close to the huge engines, and people who had paid only $10 to travel slept ten to a room. Also, more than a thousand of them had to share just two baths for the entire voyage. The baths were filled with seawater, but the ship did have the luxury of central heating. As almost no one had central heating at home in those days, that was a great treat.

Many of the richer passengers had their own bathrooms, of course, and the first-class suites looked like the very best rooms in London's finest hotels. These were on the upper

decks, which meant they were quiet and had the best views of the ocean.

A few of the luxury suites were even large enough to have walk-in closets and a separate sitting room. Rich passengers could ask a member of the crew to run a bath for them, or get their clothes ready, or even polish their shoes. A crew member came in every morning to change the sheets and make up the beds.

Passengers in first class had a choice of stylish restaurants and cafes. An orchestra played every day to entertain diners eating in the best restaurant (which was also the largest ever seen on a ship), and one of the cafes had real palm trees growing in huge wooden tubs.

There were all sorts of expensive treats on the *Titanic*'s menus—oysters, salmon, and turbot in lobster sauce. There was also roast duckling, spiced beef, and plover on toast (a plover is a type of rare seabird). Hundreds of bottles of wine and champagne were carried on board, for first-class passengers only, and there were more than 8,000 cigars for men who wished to smoke on deck or in the luxurious first-class smoking room.

The kitchen's enormous stores held all sorts of different foods, but when the *Titanic*'s rich passengers weren't eating or drinking, there were plenty of other things for them to do instead.

White Star Line ships were the first anywhere in the world to have heated swimming pools. The *Titanic* also had a squash racquets court and a gymnasium with a rowing machine, exercise bikes, and a punching bag. There was a beautiful Turkish Bath complex with a steam room and an electric sunbed, and there was another room where passengers could enjoy a relaxing massage. The ship also had two libraries, a ladies' writing room, and a

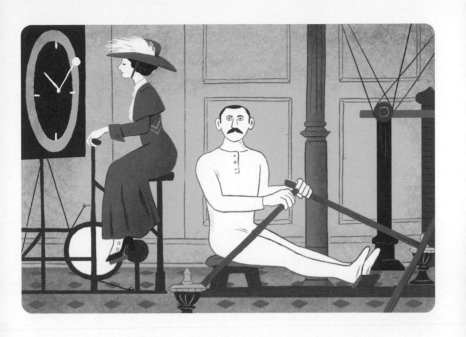

barbershop. It wasn't just a ship but a sort of floating holiday resort.

Harland and Wolff had paid very close attention to the style and decoration of the more expensive cabins and the grand public rooms. Their craftsmen had used vast amounts of marble, mahogany, sycamore, walnut, oak, and satinwood to create sweeping staircases and roomy, richly paneled saloons on the ship's upper decks. The company's designers copied different historical styles to design rooms that felt like those in an English country house, a medieval French castle, and an Italian Renaissance palace.

The attention to detail was incredible. Fine wooden paneling in the first-class smoking room had genuine mother-of-pearl inlays and colorful stained-glass windows, and many of the ship's elegant cut-glass lamps were covered in real silver. Even the wastepaper baskets in the cabins and the quilts on the beds had been specially ordered from the best suppliers the company could find.

A very large crew worked hard to keep everything polished and working on such a massive ship, and the White Star Line employed around 883 people on board the *Titanic*, 23 of whom were women. Captain Edward John Smith and a handful of senior officers were in charge of the large crew of seamen, engineers, and electricians needed to sail the ship and to keep the engines working. In addition, more than 70 "trimmers" worked day and night shoveling coal down to the boilers, while others worked full-time to clean the ship's many windows.

There were plenty of crew members to look after the passengers as well: two doctors in case anyone fell ill, musicians and barbers, a couple of professional sports instructors (for the gymnasium and squash racquets court), and even a printer who produced a daily newspaper for those passengers who wanted to catch up on the news.

More than 400 others were employed
in the ship's busy Victualling Department.
This provided all the food, housekeeping, and
laundry services, so there were hundreds
of bakers, chefs, butchers, fish dealers, and
dishwashers, as well as bedmakers and cleaners
who helped run the ship as a luxury hotel.

4

"THE SAFEST SHIPS EVER BUILT"

As well as making these new ships large and luxurious, Lord Pirrie and Thomas Andrews wanted them to be the safest vessels of their kind in the world and to reduce the risk of them sinking.

One way to do this was to make the hull as strong as possible, and so Harland and Wolff used steel that was thicker and heavier than what was used on other ships.

Then they thought about the space inside the hull. The hull of an ordinary ship is like a giant empty box. If the ship hits a rock or crashes into another ship, seawater rushes in through the hole made in the hull and then floods the space inside. This happens incredibly quickly when it is a large hole, and even a really big ship can take only a few minutes to sink once it is full of water.

Andrews and his team thought they could stop the *Titanic*'s entire hull from flooding if they divided it into 16 separate watertight compartments. Then, if only four of these compartments filled up with seawater, the *Titanic* might remain afloat. If five or six compartments flooded, Andrews knew the *Titanic* would sink in the end, but slowly. And if the *Titanic* stayed afloat for longer, other ships in the area would have time to reach it and rescue the passengers.

This was a very clever invention, but the *Titanic* and its sister ships had even more safety features.

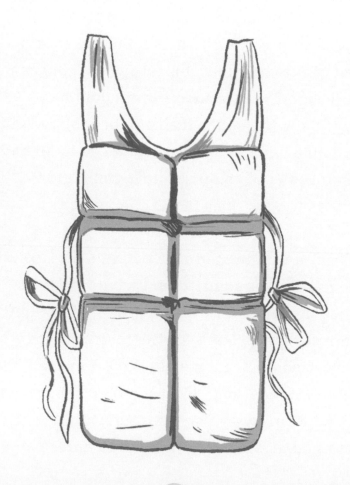

Each ship carried more than 3,500 life vests on board that were of the most modern and advanced design. They were made of cork and canvas and would keep a passenger afloat in the water even if he or she couldn't swim.

This was essential because most people were not taught to swim at this time. Although the *Titanic* had a swimming pool for the first-class passengers, many of the people on board had never been to a beach or even paddled in the sea.

When the ship was launched, a White Star Line advertisement said that the new ships had been "designed to be unsinkable," but Harland and Wolff still needed to build sturdy wooden lifeboats for them.

The *Olympic*, the *Britannic*, and the *Titanic* each had room on their decks for 64 lifeboats and the davits (a type of crane) needed to lower them down into the water.

This was far more than most ships had at the time, and so the *Titanic* was finally fitted with only 20 of them before she set sail.

Lifeboats and davits take up a lot of space. The directors of the White Star Line thought their passengers would prefer to have more room to move around on deck and to play games.

But this meant there would not be enough lifeboats for everyone if something did go wrong during a voyage.

The *Titanic* also had something called a Marconi Room. This was named after an Italian engineer who had invented a way for people to send messages to each other by radio. Rich passengers could pay to send what were known as "Marconigrams" to their friends and families. Businessmen could also use these to stay in touch with their companies while they were at sea.

The complex equipment in the room needed a specially trained radio operator to use it properly, and it was incredibly expensive. To send even a short ten-word message cost what would be about $94 in today's money.

Marconi's radio equipment had another, more important purpose too. Without a radio, ships at sea had to communicate with each other using codes that needed different

colored flags or flashing lights. This was called semaphore signaling. But flags were no good in the dark or over very long distances. Even the brightest light was no good if a ship was too far away to be seen.

Radio changed all that, and so for its new ships the White Star Line ordered the most powerful transmitter that Marconi's company could make.

With this transmitter, a radio operator could send a distress signal hundreds of miles from a sinking ship, or the captain could warn other ships in the area if he had spotted something dangerous floating in the sea, such as an iceberg.

Because the radio was so important, the Marconi Room worked 24 hours a day. Most of the time, the two radio operators sent and received expensive Marconigrams for the passengers. However, the radio operators also took navigation messages for the captain and listened for weather reports and iceberg warnings.

Icebergs were a major danger to ships crossing the cold waters of the North Atlantic, so the crew of the *Titanic* also included six men called "lookouts."

The lookouts worked in pairs and kept watch day and night from the crow's nest. A lookout's job was to ring a brass bell as loudly as possible if they spotted an iceberg or saw another ship that was sailing too close.

5

SETTING SAIL FOR AMERICA

A ship's first voyage is called its maiden voyage. There is nothing more exciting than when a new ship sets sail for the first time. When the *Titanic* sailed out of a special new deep-water dock at Southampton, in southern

England, just before lunchtime on April 10, 1912, thousands of people were there to wave her off.

Many of the passengers on board had come down to the coast that morning by special train from London's Waterloo Station. The *Titanic*'s next port of call was Cherbourg in France so that more passengers could come on board. The following morning the ship also

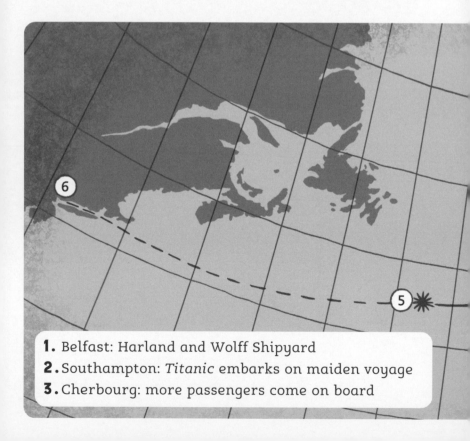

1. Belfast: Harland and Wolff Shipyard
2. Southampton: *Titanic* embarks on maiden voyage
3. Cherbourg: more passengers come on board

stopped at Queenstown in southern Ireland to pick up 123 extra passengers. After this, the captain and crew got ready to steam nonstop across the Atlantic for more than 3,000 miles.

When the *Titanic* left the port at Queenstown (now known as Cobh) the decks were crowded, but the ship was not completely full. No one knows exactly how many passengers and

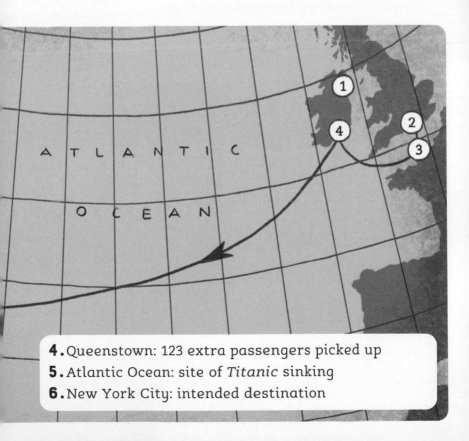

4. Queenstown: 123 extra passengers picked up
5. Atlantic Ocean: site of *Titanic* sinking
6. New York City: intended destination

crew were on board, but it is believed to have been around 2,200 men, women, and children. About 883 of these were crew members. The remaining 1,317 were fare-paying passengers heading for New York City. Just over 100 of them were young children traveling with their parents.

Third-class passengers were mostly migrants leaving Europe, poor families who were looking to start a new (and hopefully better) life in America. Their lives were very different from those of the passengers in first class.

Many of the first-class passengers were famous as well as very rich. Captain Smith welcomed them on board personally. There was millionaire John Jacob Astor IV, who was one of the world's wealthiest businessmen, and a fashionable clothes designer called Lady Duff-Gordon. Francis Davis Millet and Paul Chevré were both successful artists, Karl Behr and Dick Williams were champion tennis

players, and Elsie Bowerman later became a well-known campaigner for women's rights. Film producer Pierre Maréchal was one of the first men in France to pilot an airplane.

The White Star Line's managing director, Joseph Bruce Ismay, was also on board for this exciting maiden voyage. He and the *Titanic*'s designer, Thomas Andrews, wanted to see how well the ship performed and to make sure there were no problems to upset their passengers.

To their horror, there was an incident before the *Titanic* had even made its way out of Southampton harbor. Before the voyage had really even begun, a potentially terrible accident was only narrowly avoided.

Every vessel churns up the water as it moves along. Water in front of the hull is pushed along in what is known as a bow wave. Behind it, other waves fan out to create what sailors call a wash.

A canoe or a small rowing boat doesn't disturb the water too much, but a ship as large as the *Titanic* can actually make smaller vessels capsize or sink. Even quite large ships can be dangerously battered by waves from a much larger one, and this is what happened to an American ocean liner that was tied up in Southampton harbor.

The *City of New York* was elegant and fast
and quite large, but it weighed less than half as
much as the *Titanic*. As the *Titanic* passed by,
this much lighter vessel was lifted up by a great

wave and then dropped back into the water as the wave moved on.

The sudden shock of this snapped the strong steel cables that were holding the *City of New York* in position. The noise sounded like a gun going off, and the rear end of the ship (the stern) began to swing out toward the *Titanic*.

Captain Smith immediately ordered the *Titanic*'s powerful engines to be put "full astern," which means that the engines went into reverse. At the same time, a quick-thinking tugboat crew managed to attach a new cable to the *City of New York* and tow it back into position. A potentially deadly accident was avoided by a few seconds. At one point, the two ships had been just 4 feet apart. Had they hit each other, the result could have been disastrous.

A day later, as the *Titanic* steamed out into the Atlantic, the weather was warm, although

there were a few clouds and a stiff breeze.
A small fire had broken out in one of the vast
coal stores, but this often happened on these
early steamships. It wasn't as dangerous as
it sounds, and the crew had it under control
before any of the passengers knew what was
going on.

Most of the passengers just settled down to
enjoy the weeklong voyage and the wonderful
experience of sailing on the world's largest,
most luxurious passenger ship. A few of them
would have suffered from seasickness and
stayed in their cabins. But for the others, there
was plenty of room to move around (especially
in first and second class) and much to do to
pass the time.

As well as the restaurants, libraries,
pool, and gym, there were deck games, which
everyone enjoyed. Card games, chess, and
backgammon matches were also available for
the less energetic.

Passengers only mixed with others in the same class as their own, but life on board a transatlantic liner was very friendly and a lot of fun. As the *Titanic* steamed onward, there were lavish dinners and many parties, music from the orchestra (and from the piano in third class), and time to enjoy all that such a luxurious ship had to offer, as well as the ocean views and the crossing itself. The passengers who could afford it sent more than 200 Marconigrams to their friends and families back home.

6

DISASTER STRIKES

While all the passengers were enjoying themselves, the *Titanic*'s crew was working hard and the ship was making impressive headway through the waves of the North Atlantic. Captain Smith wasn't trying to break any records for speed, but after the first day's sailing the ship was already 557 miles from Queenstown, Ireland.

The next day, the *Titanic* traveled 597 miles, and the day after that another 628. By this time it was much colder outside, but there was no wind. The sea around the *Titanic*'s hull was clear and calm but cold.

Sailors all know that icebergs are a serious problem for ships crossing the Atlantic. Every year, more than 1,000 icebergs slowly drift down from the frozen waters of the Arctic, and hundreds of others drift up into the Atlantic from Antarctica. It was no different in 1912.

The largest iceberg ever recorded in the Atlantic, in 2000, was an astonishing 183 miles long and more than 20 miles wide. That's about the same size as Jamaica, and half the size of Wales. Scientists think that it must have weighed more than 110 trillion tons. Even a much smaller iceberg can easily sink a ship if the two of them crash.

Many of the icebergs in the North Atlantic have broken off from the giant glaciers of Greenland. In 1912, as the *Titanic* made its way across the ocean, it was impossible to spot even the largest iceberg at night because radar had not yet been invented.

By the time an iceberg was near enough to be seen by anyone on a ship, it was much too late to stop or steer away from it. And even in daylight, when you can see the top of an iceberg easily, the real danger comes from what lies under the surface of the water, hidden and unseen.

Ships' captains and lookouts used to cooperate with one another to help watch out for icebergs. They might be working for rival shipping companies, but nobody wanted to hear that another ship had sunk or that passengers and crew members had lost their lives.

Luckily the invention of radio made it possible for a ship to warn others in the area if any ice had been spotted, and on April 14, the *Titanic*'s Marconi Room received a number of urgent warnings. Several large icebergs had drifted farther south than usual. One had been seen in the area, and the *Titanic* was heading straight for it.

The White Star Line had equipped its luxury ship with one of the best and most expensive radio systems in the world, but the warnings were ignored. The *Titanic* kept steaming forward through the darkness, and at 11:40 p.m., at the very moment that it hit the iceberg, the radio operator was busy sending a private message for one of the first-class passengers.

The iceberg wasn't a large one. Experts think it was only 200 to 400 feet long and between 50 and 100 feet high. But the *Titanic* was traveling fast, at about 25 miles an hour (almost its top speed), which made the impact worse.

As the ship's steel hull slid along the side of the iceberg, there was a horrible grinding sound and the whole ship shuddered. This only lasted for seconds and many passengers who were asleep in bed didn't know that anything was happening.

However, beneath the surface, a sharp and jagged spur of ice ripped into the thick metal plates of the hull. Thousands of iron rivets snapped and the steel plates bent under the force. Seawater began to flood through the gaps and into the ship's watertight compartments. The *Titanic* was still more than 1,200 miles from its destination, but Captain Smith ordered his crew to stop the engines at once.

Smith must have been horribly shocked by what had just happened. Before setting sail, he had told a reporter that he couldn't think of anything that would sink the ship. "Modern shipbuilding," he said, "has gone beyond that." Thomas Andrews had explained to him how the *Titanic* could stay afloat if as many as four of its compartments were flooded. Unfortunately, it was soon clear that at least six of those compartments were filling with water.

Also, it now turned out that the compartments weren't watertight after all. The *Titanic* did have some powerful pumps to drive the water out, but these couldn't cope with the millions of gallons of seawater that were pouring into the hull of the ship.

The weight of all this water inside the ship caused the *Titanic* to list badly, or lean over. The captain and his crew saw that their great ship was sinking. It was impossible to say how long this would take, but the more the *Titanic* listed, the more quickly the seawater rushed in.

The radio operator was instructed to stop sending passengers' Marconigrams immediately and to put out a distress message to any other ships in the area. Other members of the crew fired special rockets called flares up into the night sky. These looked like huge fireworks and were another way of signaling that help was urgently needed. Just before midnight the order was given to prepare the lifeboats.

Because nobody at the White Star Line had believed their new ship could sink or ever would, there weren't enough lifeboats for everyone on board. Even if there had been, the sinking ship was so far from land that it would have been impossible for any of the passengers to row themselves to safety.

At midnight, in the middle of the Atlantic, the only hope of survival for the 2,200 passengers and crew depended on other ships nearby. If these ships saw a flare, or heard one of the SOS messages, then they could turn around and sail to the rescue of the *Titanic*.

For more than 150 years, the rule on board a sinking ship has been "women and children first." This means places on lifeboats are reserved for them ahead of the men. But because everyone thought the *Titanic* was unsinkable, no one had explained this to passengers or shown them what to do if something went wrong.

Most of the passengers just panicked. Frightened people pushed their way onto the lifeboats instead of waiting until it was their turn. Some of the lifeboats drifted off before they were full and left other passengers stranded on the ship.

There were enough life vests for everyone on board, but anyone who put one on and jumped into the water was likely to die of the cold before help came. Many of the passengers were simply too scared to move or too shocked to think about what to do. Several of them just stood around and didn't even try to escape until it was far too late.

A couple of hours after hitting the iceberg, the front part of the *Titanic* was almost completely underwater. Now more and more water was pouring in through open doorways and hatches, and the ship was sinking even faster. At one point the stern, with its three mighty propellers,

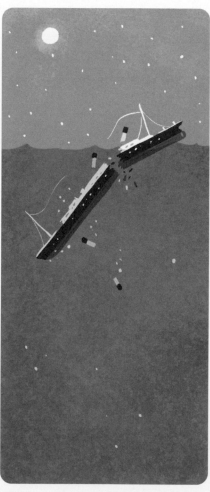

rose high into the air—a terrifying sight, especially as the ship was beginning to split into two. Seconds later, the massive ship vanished beneath the surface and plummeted more than two miles down to the ocean floor, taking hundreds and hundreds of passengers with it.

7

THE RESCUE

It's impossible to say exactly how many people went down with the ship, and there was still no sign of help for the hundreds of others who had crowded into the lifeboats or for those who were floating around in the freezing cold water. Most of the people in the sea survived for only

a few minutes. Hardly any of them were lucky
enough to be pulled into one of the lifeboats
before they died from the cold or drowned.

Around 2,200 passengers and crew had been
on the ship when it left Queenstown less than
five days earlier. Now more than two thirds of
them were dead. Those who were left alive, and
who were now drifting around in the darkness
in small wooden boats, could only hope and
pray that someone would come to rescue them.

The ship closest to the scene of the disaster was the *Californian*, but unfortunately its wireless operator had switched off his radio and gone to bed. No one on board heard the SOS message sent from the *Titanic*. Then, when a member of the crew did spot five distress flares in the distance, the captain decided not to do anything about it. Perhaps he was too worried about running his own ship into an iceberg.

Luckily, the radio operator on another ship did hear a message from the *Titanic*. Cunard's *Carpathia* had left New York a few days before and was traveling to Europe across the Atlantic. It was much too far away for anyone on deck to see the distress flares, but when the captain was told about the radio message, he ordered his ship to turn around at once. The crew was ordered to steam at full speed toward the place where the *Titanic* had gone down.

This was definitely the right thing to do, but it was also extremely dangerous. The

Carpathia had to travel nearly 60 miles in the pitch-dark to reach the survivors. Both the captain and his crew knew this would mean sailing through an area that was scattered with icebergs. They also knew that at least one of these icebergs was large enough to sink the biggest passenger ship in the world.

The *Carpathia*'s captain ordered all the heating and hot water to be switched off so that the steam and power produced by the ship's boilers could be used to travel as fast as possible. Even so, the difficult journey through the night took longer than three and a half hours. More than half of this time was spent dodging dozens of icebergs. Several extra lookouts had been posted on deck to make sure that the *Carpathia* didn't make the same mistake as the *Titanic* had.

At last, at around four o'clock in the morning, the *Carpathia* arrived in the area where the

Titanic had sunk. There was lots of debris floating in the water but no sign of the ship, which by this time was lying in pieces on the seabed.

The *Carpathia*'s crew spent the next four hours searching a large area of the ocean to find the ship's 20 lifeboats. These had drifted off in different directions, but in the end the

Carpathia found all 20 and helped to bring the shivering passengers on board their ship.

No one knows exactly how many survivors were rescued in this way, but the *Carpathia* took on board somewhere between 705 and 712 people. That was a huge number for a ship that was already crowded with its own passengers.

The passengers and crew of the *Carpathia* began handing out blankets and hot drinks as the ship made its way back to New York. Many of them crowded onto the decks to try to spot

any survivors in the freezing water. Everyone hoped a few might still be struggling to stay afloat, but sadly there were none to be seen who weren't already dead.

More than half of those lifted from the lifeboats were women and children, including a two-month-old baby girl who had been traveling in third class.

Although the rush for lifeboats had been chaotic and disorganized (and terrifying for everyone involved), many of those on board the *Titanic* had stuck to the old rule about "women and children first."

There must have been many husbands, fathers, and sons who didn't climb into any of the lifeboats even when they knew it was their only chance of survival. And at least one woman had died because she refused to leave her husband behind when she was offered a place on a lifeboat but he wasn't.

The *Carpathia* reached New York City safely three days later, but the sinking of the *Titanic* was a terrible tragedy.

Weirdly, the first news that people in London read about the *Titanic* was that no one had died and that the ship had been towed to Nova Scotia, in Canada. In fact, about 1,500 people had lost their lives in just a few hours.

The huge death toll made it the worst shipping disaster anywhere in the world at this time, and more than a hundred years later the sinking of the *Titanic* is still the worst and most famous disaster to happen to an ocean liner.

Not only had hundreds of passengers drowned, but Captain Smith had gone down with his ship as well as around 700 members of his crew. It is terrible to know that at least 50 of the dead were young children, and many of those who did survive lost their parents. One of the survivors was 15-year-old Edith Haisman, who later remembered sitting in a lifeboat waving goodbye to her father. He promised to see her in New York, but he was never seen again.

8

AFTER THE DISASTER

When people found out the truth about what had happened to the *Titanic*, and how many people had been killed, it caused shock waves not just in London and New York but around the world. Reporters and their readers were gripped by the story. Most found it far more interesting than news of any other disasters, including a terrible flood in China at about the same time that killed at least 20 times as many people.

Most people couldn't believe that such a large and modern ship as the *Titanic* had been wrecked on its first-ever voyage, or that a ship that everyone thought was unsinkable had sunk so quickly.

The names of the rich and famous who had died made the story even more interesting; also, ordinary people were amazed by all the details of the ship's incredible luxury. There was something chilling about the immense power of Nature (the iceberg) over what had been the greatest machine ever built.

It wasn't just the huge number of deaths that grabbed the imagination of readers either. Almost everything about what had happened sounded extraordinary.

Before the sinking of the *Titanic*, most people had no idea that an iceberg could be so much larger than a ship. As well as that, people read that although the *Titanic* had been fast (its top speed was 26 miles an hour), the effect of gravity meant that it actually traveled even faster as it sank, nose down, to the bottom of the Atlantic. Experts now think it must have reached approximately 35 miles an hour before finally crashing into the seabed—a terrifying thought.

For weeks after the tragedy, newspapers in Britain and elsewhere printed some amazing stories of courage and heroism, and Winston Churchill wrote to say how much he admired the way in which women and children had been allowed onto the lifeboats first.

But there was also fury and great sadness. Fury that Joseph Bruce Ismay of the White Star Line had survived (some people thought he should have stayed on board and gone down

with his ship). And sadness that so many
innocent people had died in such a horrible
way. Everyone was determined to find out
what had gone wrong in order to make sure
that nothing like it ever happened again.

The families of the dead were angry as well as upset that the *Titanic* had not had enough lifeboats. The White Star Line had not broken any laws by having only 20, but new rules were brought in to force every transatlantic liner to be equipped with enough lifeboats for everyone on board. And it became law that practice drills were carried out at the start of every voyage. Passengers had to know what to do in an emergency.

There was better training for radio operators too. And ships needed to have at least one radio operator on duty at all times to improve the reporting of hazards such as icebergs.

The last thing that happened was that efforts were made to hugely improve the way that new vessels were built. First, the watertight compartments were improved to give ships a much better chance of staying afloat after a collision and, better still, the steel rivets that were used were made harder and stronger so that hull plates didn't split apart.

You could say that although the sinking of the *Titanic* was a huge tragedy, some good came of it in the end. New ships built after the terrible events of 1912 were much safer, and many more lives must have been saved as a result.

Although it wasn't possible to start again and rebuild the hulls of the *Titanic*'s sister ships, the *Olympic* and the *Britannic*, some improvements were made to them. The *Olympic* went on to have a long career at sea and was a troop ship during the First World War. After that, it became a passenger ship and stayed in service until 1935. The *Britannic* didn't do as well. It sank, in 1916, after being struck by a German mine, and 30 lives were lost.

Both ships have been more or less forgotten, but the *Titanic* continues to grow more and more famous. Many books have been written about the disaster, and a handful of blockbuster films have thrilled and horrified moviegoers around the world.

Perhaps the most exciting thing was the discovery of the wreck in 1985 by an American oceanographer. Submarines have been able to dive down to the wreck—it is far too deep underwater for a human diver—and bring back relics from the ship.

The crews of the submarines have rescued bits of the ship as well as smaller items from the *Titanic*'s luxurious interior. Whenever anything connected to the ship comes up for sale, collectors pay enormous prices: one person paid more than $25,000 just for a photograph of the iceberg! It looks as if the *Titanic* is the one ship that no one ever wants to forget.

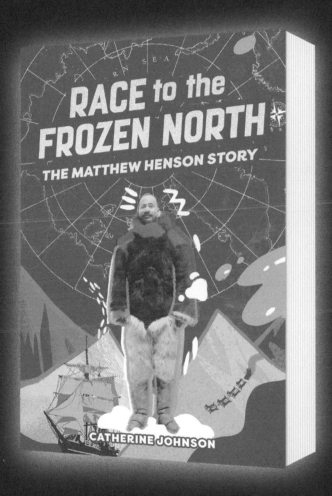

Our books are tested
for children and young people by
children and young people.

Thanks to everyone who consulted on
a manuscript for their time and effort in
helping us to make our books better
for our readers.